# THE TASHA TUDOR
# FAMILY COOKBOOK

# THE TASHA TUDOR FAMILY COOKBOOK

### Heirloom Recipes and Warm Memories from Corgi Cottage

WINSLOW TUDOR

*Find out more about Tasha Tudor at*
*www.tashatudorandfamily.com*

**Skyhorse Publishing**

Skyhorse Publishing books may be purchased in bulk at special discounts for sales promotion, corporate gifts, fund-raising, or educational purposes. Special editions can also be created to specifications. For details, contact the Special Sales Department, Skyhorse Publishing, 307 West 36th Street, 11th Floor, New York, NY 10018 or info@skyhorsepublishing.com.

Skyhorse® and Skyhorse Publishing® are registered trademarks of Skyhorse Publishing, Inc.®, a Delaware corporation.

Visit our website at www.skyhorsepublishing.com.

10 9 8 7 6 5 4 3 2 1

Library of Congress Cataloging-in-Publication Data is available on file.

Cover design by Jane Sheppard
Cover illustration by Tasha Tudor

Print ISBN: 978-1-5107-1099-3
Ebook ISBN: 978-1-5107-1100-6

Printed in China

# Table of Contents

# *Introduction*

Tasha possessed an enduring enthusiasm for her many interests, of which cooking was one of the greatest. Her pantry extended beyond the walls of her kitchen to include her vegetable garden, herb garden, eggs from her chickens, and milk from her cows and goats. She maintained an awareness of and friendship with the earth and the plants that grew on it that came through in the food she made. The preservation of her receipts and cooking methods is part of a larger picture that includes the conservation of her gardens, her house, and the many tools and objects she required for self-sufficiency. Her traditions are alive and relevant, and still a way of life on the property. Her home and gardens continue to be cherished and maintained by her son Seth and his wife Marjorie, their son Winslow and his wife Amy, and their two children Ellie and Katie.

Tasha was a great cook and baker. What did she make? How did she cook, and with what? There were three meals a day, breakfast, dinner, and supper. Nowadays we think of dinner as a big evening meal, but then dinner was lunch and people had dinner pails, now called lunch boxes. Tasha had a number of special cooking utensils and accessories. One of the most important was her vanilla bottle, which she always refilled partway with store vanilla—partway because it would take several bottles to fill. It was such an important

thing to her. She had a large flour sifter with a crank handle, and a small one that you held and shook the handle back and forth. Her corn bread irons were central to many meals.

Up until the 1960s she used aluminum pots, colanders, and measuring cups, as well as cast-iron frying pans. Later on she used copper kettles, pots and pans, glass measuring cups, and continued to use cast iron. She always used a small three-minute hourglass, wooden spoons, an old black French chef's knife, yellow ware bowls, bean crocks, a rolling pin, whisks, hand-cranked eggbeaters, chopping boards, a tin kitchen, and nutmeg graters. She had an apple corer and various small glass and china bowls for individual custards. She used a meat grinder quite often to make leftover meat—such as ham, chicken, or turkey—into croquettes, but more often for carrot salad. She never had a cake stand and instead served cake on a big round plate. She had boxes of birthday candles, cooling racks, cookie sheets, and cake pans with removable bottoms. Nothing out of the ordinary, but pretty much every-thing in her kitchen she had most of her life. For instance, while exploring an abandoned house with her father in the 1920s, she found an old potato masher, and used it for the next eight decades.

Since there were usually two or three cows, later replaced by goats, there was a lot of milk, heavy

Winslow Tudor

cream, and butter. Tasha always kept chickens. At times there were omelets to use excess eggs. Every morning for breakfast she squeezed orange juice and served eggs, sausage, or cereals like oatmeal, Cream of Wheat, or Maltex. Cold cereals were also popular: cornflakes, shredded wheat, puffed oats, and All-Bran. She often made pancakes served with maple syrup and plenty of bacon. Interestingly, Spam was sometimes used, fried, usually for breakfast instead of sausage or bacon. Sometimes the Cream of Wheat was made the day before so it was fairly hard, cut into strips, and fried until brown and served on a plate with maple syrup.

There was beef, pork, lamb, ham, chicken, and occasionally fish. Beef was in the form of roasts, steaks, or hamburgers. On rare occasions there was lamb with mint sauce, or ham roasted with cloves. Chicken was stewed or roasted. Some of the meat was raised on the farm, and other times she bought it. Beef stew was always good, along with homemade baked beans and wheat bread. She made very rich corn bread in iron pans, served with butter and jam. When it got a little stale it was cut in half and fried. There was never any hard alcohol, beer, or wine in the house.

Vegetables from the summer garden included lettuce, tomatoes, corn, broccoli, spinach, chard, Brussels sprouts (not popular), cabbage, cauliflower, beets, kale, carrots, peas, beans, squash, potatoes, and onions. In winter if she ran out of vegetables from the big chest freezer, she would buy commercial stuff.

There were always a lot of desserts and sweets around. Apple pies, oatmeal cookies, baked custard served out into saucers, fudge, puddings, often chocolate pudding served cold with heavy cream, chocolate chip cookies, brownies, sugar cookies, and rice pudding with raisins. There were cakes, usually two layer, ice cream with homemade chocolate sauce, and baked apples filled with brown sugar and raisins. The brown sugar melted and made sticky syrup in the pan, and was later poured over the apples.

Tasha made crackers and baking powder biscuits, but also bought soda crackers, graham crackers, Fig Newtons, Oreos, and Ritz Crackers, peppermints, Junior Mints, and Milky Way bars. And "refrigerator cookies," which were store-bought, round or square, thin, plain chocolate cookies assembled in a pile with whipped cream in each layer, refrigerated until softened, with chocolate syrup over the top. She made punch, tea, cider, and root beer.

Tasha traveled a great deal. Locally, she went to Boston, New Haven, Pittsfield, New York City, Connecticut, and along the way ate at Howard Johnsons and Schrafft's in Boston. Traveling also meant picnics with sandwiches made from thin slices of bread and filled with chopped hard-boiled egg, mayonnaise (always Hellmann's), and chopped bacon, or marshmallow and peanut butter, or chopped pickle and mayonnaise, or jelly, or sliced beef or chicken. She spent a lot of time in the kitchen and her gardens, and she put it this way: "I love to cook, and don't mind doing the dishes."

The continued interest of Tasha by the many people who got to know her either in person or through her appealing, detailed watercolors and stories is a vital component to her legacy. She felt deep gratitude for her fans and never missed an opportunity to thank them for their support of her art.

# Breads and Muffins

✧

# Baking Powder Biscuits

### Makes 18 2-inch biscuits

Baking powder biscuits tend to show up most often at breakfast. They are good with jam and butter. Yet they do very well at lunch when baked with a slice of cheese between two flat dough cutouts. Their usefulness extends to strawberry shortcake, too. They attain greater height while baking if cut from dough versus dropped in mounds on a baking sheet. Tasha did both, and they tasted the same. She rolled the dough on a small, yellow, free-standing marble-top counter.

The more dough is worked, the tougher biscuits are. Tasha observed the addition of an egg to baking powder biscuits was prevalent in New England, but less so in the Southern states.

| | |
|---|---|
| 1 egg | 4 teaspoons baking powder |
| ½–¾ cup milk | ½ teaspoon salt |
| 2 cups all-purpose flour | 6 tablespoons butter |

Preheat oven to 450°F.

Whisk together egg and milk in small bowl. In separate large bowl, combine flour, baking powder, and salt.

Cut butter into marble-size pieces and mix lightly into flour with hands. Add milk and egg mixture. Mix minimally with fork until ingredients are barely combined.

Press dough out onto counter with hands, then roll to ½-inch thickness. Cut straight down with sharp biscuit cutter.

Bake 8–12 minutes or until just browned on top. Makes about a dozen biscuits.

# Banana Bread

8 servings

Banana bread was more of a traveling or picnic food, and less a regular menu item for Tasha. Spring in New England meant day-long excursions to plant nurseries in Vermont, New Hampshire, Massachusetts, Connecticut, and sometimes New York State. The day before the trip was spent packing a really good lunch with plenty of snacks for the drive there and back. We usually arrived a little before noon at the farthest places, parked in the shade, and set up a picnic blanket in a quiet corner of a display garden. Tasha brought hot tea in a thermos bottle and a wicker picnic basket that held six cups, six plates, banana bread, deviled eggs, brownies, fruit, and six pearl-handled knives to spread jam or butter on cracker sandwiches. Many years have gone by since these trips now, and a lot of the nurseries Tasha frequented are gone. Some are not, however, and the trees that provided shade during picnics are still there and doing well. Tasha always had wonderful stories to tell during the drive, and endless enthusiasm for the nurseries, the proprietors, her traveling companions, the plants, and getting back home.

6 tablespoons butter

½ cup sugar

2 eggs

1½ cups all-purpose flour

½ teaspoon salt

½ teaspoon baking powder

½ teaspoon baking soda

2 ripe bananas

Preheat oven to 350°F.

In a large bowl place warm, almost-melted butter. Add sugar, eggs, then remaining ingredients. Mix well.

Bake in well-greased bread pan for 45–50 minutes, or until fork inserted in top center comes out clean.

# Blueberry Muffins

## Makes 18 muffins

The high quantity and broad distribution of blueberry bushes around the periphery of Tasha's garden is a source of delight for the birds. Yet this planting technique is such that here and there an entire blueberry bush is overlooked or unheeded by blue jays and robins. Tasha put these blueberries straight into blueberry muffins, pies, or the freezer for later use. Many lowbush blueberries inhabit the fringe of fields and wild spaces adjacent to Tasha's garden, and were prized by her for use in jams and muffins.

2 cups all-purpose flour

½ teaspoon salt

1 tablespoon baking powder

¾ cup sugar

½ cup shortening or butter

2 eggs

¾ cup milk

1 teaspoon vanilla extract

1 cup blueberries

Preheat oven to 400°F.

Combine flour, salt, baking powder, and sugar. Add shortening or butter, eggs, milk, and vanilla extract, and mix until barely combined. Fold blueberries into batter.

Grease muffin pan, and spoon batter in, about ⅔ full. Sprinkle tops with sugar and cinnamon if desired.

Bake 20 minutes or until just browned and fork comes out clean.

# Bran Muffins

### Makes 24 small muffins

Prior to the 1980s, Tasha made bran muffins from a receipt that varies from the one she used later. Both are good. This is the pre-1980s version, a breakfast staple for the first sixty-five years of Tasha's life. Bran muffins are durable. They travel well, store well, and are nourishing, filling, and invariably welcomed by visitors. Tasha kept unused batter refrigerated in a crock covered by a plate for up to a week, and would make as many as needed to suit the occasion, from two to a dozen. She collected eggs in the evening and stored them overnight on the plate covering the bran muffin batter, to sort the following morning.

2 cups crushed bran flakes

2 cups all-purpose flour

¼ cup sugar

1½ teaspoons baking soda

½ teaspoon salt

4 tablespoons very soft butter

2 cups buttermilk

2 eggs

¼ cup molasses

½ cup raisins

Preheat oven to 400°F.

In a large mixing bowl, combine crushed bran flakes, flour, sugar, baking soda, and salt. Mix in butter, buttermilk, eggs, molasses, and raisins.

Bake 20–25 minutes in greased muffin pan.

# Cinnamon Raisin Bread

Makes 2 8½- × 4½-inch loaves

One of Tasha's favorite quotes is from Henry David Thoreau. "If one advances confidently in the direction of his dreams, and endeavors to live the life which he has imagined, he will meet with a success unexpected in common hours." She was also fond of the rumor he had invented cinnamon raisin bread, though knew from receipts in cookbooks published prior to his time that he hadn't. Tasha toasted slices of cinnamon raisin bread for tea, or had it untoasted with butter for breakfast.

2 tablespoons active dry yeast

⅓ cup water at 100–110°F

2 cups milk at 100–110°F

6 tablespoons soft butter, plus 1 tablespoon for greasing pans and loaves

4 teaspoons sugar

2 eggs

2 teaspoons salt

6 cups all-purpose flour

1 cup raisins

2 tablespoons cinnamon

¼ cup cinnamon-sugar

In a large bowl, mix yeast and water. Let stand for several minutes. Add milk, butter, sugar, eggs, salt, and flour. Knead for 10 minutes or so and allow to rise and double in size. Place raisins in a saucepan with 3 cups of water, bring to a boil, drain, and cool.

Cut dough in half. Take one half and roll out to 8 inches wide by 24–30 inches long. Coat surface with butter. Combine cinnamon and cinnamon-sugar. Sprinkle half of sugar mixture on dough, then half of raisins on dough.

Roll up dough lengthwise to form loaf, seal edges and ends of loaf, and place seam side down in greased bread pan. Repeat with remaining dough. Let rise until double in size, about 1 hour in a 75°F location.

Bake at 350°F for 45 minutes or until thermometer in center of loaf reads 170°F.

# Clover Rolls

## Makes 24 rolls

This receipt plays many roles when making menus. A clover roll is merely three small balls of bread dough baked together in a muffin pan. After baking they are easily separated into three pieces, and their manageable size is useful around a busy or crowded table. Tasha often made these rolls with extra dough from other bread receipts. She had affection for this receipt's name, as she often found four-leaf clovers when she walked through clover patches. She pressed them between pages of the books in her library and it is easier to find them there than out in the lawns. Once she found a seven-leaf clover and hung it in a small frame on her east bedroom wall.

| | |
|---|---|
| 1 tablespoon yeast | 2 teaspoons sugar |
| ¼ cup water at 100–110°F | 1 egg |
| 1 cup milk at 100–110°F | 1 teaspoon salt |
| 4 tablespoons soft butter | 3 cups all-purpose flour |

In a large bowl, mix yeast and warm water. Let stand for several minutes. Add milk, butter, sugar, eggs, salt, and flour. Knead 10 minutes or so. Let rise until double in size.

Knock down and divide into twelve sections. Now divide each of those into three more and roll into balls. Coat lightly with butter. Place three balls in each muffin cup.

Allow to rise about 30 minutes in a 75°F location, then bake in 350°F oven 12–15 minutes.

# Corn Bread

## 12 servings

This corn bread receipt has remained unchanged for generations. The most important step to follow is the careful incorporation of egg whites into the batter; otherwise the results will be less like corn bread and more like muffins. Corn bread baked in cast-iron muffin pans achieves an ideal exterior texture and is best eaten fresh. If it goes stale, cut lengthwise and toast, or heat in a skillet with a little butter and serve with maple syrup. Tasha made corn bread at either noon or supper and served it with a small bowl of strawberry or raspberry jam. She reliably received sincere compliments on this receipt's excellence.

½ cup butter

½ cup sugar

2 eggs, separated

1 cup milk

1 cup all-purpose flour

1 cup cornmeal

3 teaspoons baking powder

½ teaspoon salt

All ingredients should be at room temperature. Preheat oven to 400°F.

Combine butter and sugar, then egg yolks. Mix in milk, flour, cornmeal, baking powder, and salt. In separate bowl, beat egg whites until stiff, then fold into batter.

Spoon batter into greased muffin pan and bake 20–25 minutes.

Best served hot, either plain or with jam, butter, or maple syrup.

# Oatmeal Bread

Makes 2 8½- × 11½-inch loaves

The high percentage of oatmeal in this bread is uncommon for such a receipt. Tasha made it regularly, and emphasized the requirement to use bread flour and knead the dough thoroughly, as doing so was one of the determining factors for proper rise. As a rule, Tasha did not waste food, and often made this receipt when extra oatmeal remained in the pot after breakfast.

| | |
|---|---|
| 1⅓ cups steel-cut oats | 2 cups old-fashioned rolled oats |
| 3½ cups boiling water | 4 cups bread flour |
| ½ cup brown sugar | ½ cup dry milk |
| 8 tablespoons butter | 4 teaspoons active dry yeast |
| 2½ teaspoons salt | |

Add steel-cut oats to boiling water. Cook over medium heat, stirring occasionally until all water is absorbed. Add brown sugar, butter, and salt. Transfer to large bowl and add rolled oats, 1 cup of bread flour, and dry milk. Stir until ingredients are combined, then cover and let sit for about an hour.

Stir in yeast and remaining bread flour. Knead thoroughly. Dough will be sticky. Let rise for an hour in warm room.

Grease two standard-size bread pans, divide dough in half, shape to fit pans, and let rise until dough is 1 to 2 inches above rim.

Bake at 350°F for 40 minutes or so, or until thermometer reads 180°F in center of loaf.

The dry milk may be substituted for ½ cup flour, and half of the water replaced with milk.

The Tasha Tudor Family Cookbook

# Salted Crackers

## Makes 24 2-inch crackers

These crackers store well and are good to have on hand. Tasha kept crackers in a large, old red tea tin on the main kitchen counter next to the spice drawers, and brought them out for tea parties and lunch or ate them between meals with ham spread. The dough may be cut into squares, stamped out with cookie cutters, or formed into small balls and rolled thin. It's important to roll them to $1/8$–$1/16$ of an inch, and not apply too much coarse salt. Although this receipt is useful only for making crackers, most bread dough rolled thin and baked will turn into crackers as well.

| | |
|---|---|
| 1½ cups all-purpose flour | 2 tablespoons cold butter |
| 2 teaspoons sugar | ½ cup milk |
| ½ teaspoon salt | Coarse salt |
| ¼ teaspoon baking powder | |

Preheat oven to 425°F. In a large bowl, mix flour, sugar, salt, and baking powder. Add butter and use hands to combine. Add milk.

Mix until dough forms and knead briefly on floured surface. The dough spreads out more easily if separated into several smaller balls.

Roll out to ⅛ inch or less. Sprinkle coarse salt on dough and run rolling pin over to press it in.

Cut crackers into desired shape, prick each several times with fork, and bake until light brown.

# Wheat Bread

### Makes 3 4½– × 8½–inch loaves

Ralph Waldo Emerson authored many quotes Tasha approved of. "Life is not so short but that there is always time for courtesy" is one she humorously altered to, "Life is not so short but that there is always time to make bread."

This receipt makes three large loaves. It is entirely possible to make this out of 100 percent wheat so long as the berries have been ground very finely and the finished dough is very soft, thus allowing rising. If you do this, use about a half cup less water.

| | |
|---|---|
| 2 cups milk | 6 cups bread flour |
| 3 cups water | ¾ cup sugar |
| 3 tablespoons active dry yeast | 2 tablespoons salt |
| 6 cups whole-wheat flour | ¾ cup vegetable oil or butter |

In 2-quart or larger pot, warm milk and water to 110°F. Stir in yeast.

In a large mixing bowl, place whole-wheat flour, bread flour, sugar, salt, and vegetable oil or butter. Knead thoroughly for 10 minutes. Let rise until double in size.

Grease three bread pans. Punch down dough and cut into three sections. Shape dough to evenly fit pans. Cover with light cloth and let rise for about an hour or until 1 to 2 inches above top of pan.

Place in 350°F oven for 40 minutes, until loaves sound hollow when tapped, or thermometer reads 165°F from center top.

Bread will continue to bake a little after coming out of the oven. Remove from pans and let cool on rack.

# Breakfast

✦

# Apple Dumplings

### 6 servings

Apple dumplings make good breakfast fare. They are also an excellent dessert served with vanilla ice cream. Sometimes when Tasha made apple pie she'd also make extra pie crust dough and wrap apples in 5-inch squares. It's hard to make too many. The sugar and water mixture will thicken by the time the dumplings are done, and may be scooped from the baking dish and poured over each dumpling as it sits on a dessert plate.

2 cups all-purpose flour

2½ teaspoons baking powder

½ teaspoon salt

⅔ cup shortening

½ cup milk

2 cups brown sugar

2 cups water

¼ cup butter

½ teaspoon cinnamon

Preheat oven to 350°F.

Sift together flour, baking powder, and salt. Add shortening and cut in. Stir in milk.

On floured surface, roll out dough and cut into squares. Place a section of peeled apple in the center of each square, then sprinkle each with a mixture of ¼ teaspoon cinnamon and 1 teaspoon sugar. Press dough around apple.

Bring brown sugar, water, butter, and cinnamon to a boil. Pour over dumplings and bake for ½ hour or until done.

# Cream of Wheat

## 2 servings

Sometimes a layer of solidified Cream of Wheat remained at the bottom of the pot after breakfast. Tasha refrigerated it overnight. The next morning, she cut it into strips, fried them in a bit of butter, and served them hot on a plate beside a fork and pitcher of maple syrup. This was not an uncommon breakfast, and is a good use for leftover cereal. Sometimes she whisked an egg yolk left over from another receipt into the Cream of Wheat as it cooked. Although Cream of Wheat takes 2½ minutes to cook, once in a while Tasha remarked that it took twice as long in the 1940s.

| | |
|---|---|
| 2 cups water or milk | ¼ teaspoon salt |
| ⅓ cup Cream of Wheat | ½ tablespoon butter |

Slowly pour Cream of Wheat into boiling water or milk, stirring constantly. Add salt. Continue stirring until thick, about 2 minutes.

When cool, cut into strips. Add butter to skillet and heat until melted. Place strips in skillet and cook until browned on bottom. Flip to brown on other side.

Serve immediately with maple syrup.

# Oatmeal

1 serving

This was probably Tasha's most frequent breakfast. She cooked different types of oatmeal: sometimes steel cut or crushed, but usually rolled. In winter she made oatmeal on the woodstove, but used an electric burner in summer even though she usually started a fire in the woodstove each morning year-round. She lit the fires during summer to take the early morning chill off, and as they were small and she let them go out shortly after, the electric stove was more practical for cooking. To cook oatmeal exactly the way she did requires goat milk. For decades she kept and milked Nubian goats, and attributed her longevity to goat milk. A recently emptied oatmeal pot was immediately filled with soapy water, or cleaned and put away.

1 cup milk or water

½ cup rolled oats

Dash of salt

Bring milk or water to boil. Add oats and salt. Stir occasionally over low heat until cooked, about 5 minutes or so. Sweeten with brown sugar or maple syrup.

# Omelet

## 1 serving

Although Tasha made scrambled eggs for breakfast, were she to make an omelet it would be in the evening. The filling was invariably modest: a bit of cheese, ham, bacon, or a few pieces of tomato. She ate in the rocking chair by the fender of the cookstove, and afterward usually took her dogs for a walk. On her return she walked through the barn and closed the large south-facing double doors, the back barn door, and the door by the dovecote. This was also the time of day she did a final check on the goats and chickens, and invariably spent considerable time seeing to their well-being.

| | |
|---|---|
| 2 eggs | Pinch of salt |
| 1 tablespoon milk | 1 tablespoon butter |

Whisk eggs, milk, and salt until blended.

Over medium heat, coat 6-inch frying pan with butter.

Pour mixture and tilt pan from side to side until egg is evenly distributed. Place filling on one side of omelet, fold other side onto it, and serve right away.

# Potato Cakes

### Makes 12 1½-inch potato cakes

Tasha planted storage potatoes between the stream and main vegetable garden east of the house just below the hollyhock bank. In the slightly acidic soil the potatoes grew with few blemishes. As the nights lengthened and the first frost neared, Tasha would dig a few potatoes from the ground in the evening's waning light with a five-prong garden fork to see how the crop had turned out. The next sunny morning all the potatoes would be dug and left to cure in the sun. This toughened their skins and they'd last for months in cold storage. She stored potatoes in bushel baskets covered with burlap bags in the front hall near the library. By the time late winter and early spring arrived she usually ran out of potatoes or they'd have gone soft and sent up shoots. When she bought potatoes—or any other tuber, for that matter—from the grocery store, she picked not the largest specimen but the heaviest for its size.

Leftover mashed potatoes make good potato cakes. But potato cakes turn out better if made from scratch.

| | |
|---|---|
| 3 medium-size baking potatoes | ½–1 teaspoon salt |
| 4 eggs | Oil or butter |

Peel and then grate potatoes and wring out as much moisture as possible. You should have about 4 cups of grated potatoes. Add eggs and salt.

Fry ¼-inch patties in plenty of oil or butter until brown on both sides, about 5 minutes.

Applesauce is one of Potato Cakes' better companions. Serve hot.

# Swirled Egg

## 1 serving

This method of cooking an egg resembles poaching an egg, but is boiled, not simmered, and the yolk is cooked through, not left soft. It is important to use a fresh egg, for it will stay compact while cooking in water, while the whites of an egg that is not fresh will spin off and prove less appealing. It is better to use a wide and deep pot to allow the whirlpool of water to keep momentum while the egg initially cooks. A fresh egg that has been hard-boiled is difficult to peel and this is the way Tasha got around that problem.

Water

1 egg

Fill a pot 2 inches deep or more with water and bring to a boil.

Crack egg into a small bowl.

Stir water in brisk circular motion to create a whirlpool. Gently tip egg into center of whirlpool. Reduce heat slightly so water does not boil excessively. There is no need to stir water any more.

Egg will cook through in about 10–12 minutes. Goes well with toasted wheat bread.

# *Rice Breakfast*

2 servings

Often a summer breakfast, this dish incorporates leftover rice. This receipt came about when it was discovered there was no more oatmeal left. The toppings are suitable for many breakfast cereals.

| | |
|---|---|
| 1 small apple | ¼ cup raisins |
| 2 cups cooked rice | ½ teaspoon cinnamon |
| 2 cups milk | A little salt |
| ¼ cup brown sugar | |

Core, quarter, and dice apple. Add to rice. Add milk, brown sugar, raisins, cinnamon, and salt. Cook over low heat for 10 minutes.

# Pancakes and Waffles

## Makes 10 5–inch cakes

This is a standby receipt and makes excellent pancakes and waffles. Tasha always commented on how the same receipt turned out differently when different people made it, and how sometimes baking is 20 percent ingredients and 80 percent technique. But success for this receipt is dependent on very finely ground wheat berries. The flour should feel silky between the fingers without a trace of grittiness. When making waffles, not pancakes, the addition of extra butter to the batter improves them. How much butter is up to you, but a total of as much as 16 tablespoons is possible.

1½ cups whole-wheat flour

¼ teaspoon salt

2 teaspoons baking powder

2 tablespoons sugar

2 eggs

1½ cups milk

4 tablespoons melted butter

In a large bowl, combine whole-wheat flour, salt, baking powder, and sugar. Add eggs, milk, and butter. Mix briefly. Let sit a minute or two.

Spoon batter onto preheated, greased griddle, on medium-low heat.

Cook until one side is light brown and flip. Cook until other side is light brown.

**Vegan/gluten-free pancakes:**

Instead of milk, substitute 1½ cups applesauce. Skip the eggs. Most gluten-free flours serve as an effective replacement. Substitute oil for butter. The pancakes turn out a little differently and taste like applesauce, but are good.

# Lunch and Supper

# Asparagus Spears

4 servings

To establish an asparagus bed that provides a reliable annual crop requires persistence and patience. Tasha's asparagus patch was prolific. When she started an asparagus bed, she acquired two- or three-year-old roots, planted them in well-drained soil with plenty of compost, and waited two years before cutting any spears. To prolong the harvest, she mulched the bed heavily in fall and, when spring came, pulled the mulch away from just part of the bed. This allowed the sun to warm the exposed bed and send asparagus shoots up sooner.

1 pound asparagus

Water

Butter

Tasha prepared asparagus two ways.

The first: Stand a bunch of asparagus in an inch of water, cover, and steam 5–8 minutes, depending on size. Overcooked asparagus looks dull, but properly cooked asparagus is bright green.

The second: Chop a bundle of asparagus into 1-inch pieces, and boil in salted water 4–6 minutes. Hollandaise sauce or vinaigrette goes well with asparagus, but Tasha usually just put a little butter on it.

# *Baked Beans*

### 6 servings

This basic baked bean receipt is excellent on its own, yet accepts additional ingredients to suit individual tastes. As a catchall it especially benefits from the addition of extra sausage or bacon. Tasha often made baked beans during the colder months when the cookstove ran regularly and it was a simple matter to put a bean pot in the oven in the morning and let the contents bake until supper. She used traditional old brown bean pots, and it was a common sight to see the stove's oven door ajar and a bean pot inside with a wooden spoon sticking out. Tasha had many baked bean receipts; this is one of the most basic and oft used.

| | |
|---|---|
| 2 cups navy beans | 1½ teaspoons salt |
| 8 ounces sausage | 2 tablespoons sugar |
| 1 teaspoon mustard | 2 tablespoons molasses |

Wash beans and pick over. Soak overnight in 2 quarts water.

Simmer 1–2 hours. Drain and mix in remaining ingredients.

Add water enough to just cover beans. Bake in covered bean pot at 300°F for 6–7 hours. Add a little water if beans begin to dry out.

# *Baked Potato*

## 1 serving

One way to determine the age of a potato is to try to rub the skin off. If the skin rubs off, the potato has been recently dug. New potatoes don't bake well regardless of variety, as they have not sat long enough to become starchy, but are excellent boiled in their jackets. Starchy potatoes make for good baked potatoes. Russet potatoes bake well and are a variety Tasha planted at the beginning of May, four weeks before the average last frost for her garden. She bought seed potatoes, cut them up, doused them with sulfur, and planted them the next day. She planted Kennebec and Red Norland at the beginning of June, and these were her storage potatoes. After Tasha had planted her vegetable garden, beautiful mild weather usually prevailed until the end of May and the appearance of a full moon, at which point a killing frost visited. By then the potatoes had poked a few leaves out, and Tasha hoed earth over them to keep the frost off.

1 medium potato

Olive oil

Preheat oven to 400°F. Coat whole potato in olive oil. Pierce skin several times with fork so potato does not explode while baking. Place on oven rack and bake for 45 minutes to an hour, depending on size. Let potato cool a little, cut lengthwise, and add a little bit of salted butter or sour cream.

# *Bean Stew*

4–6 servings

This was a good and oft-repeated winter lunch, cooked in a large, deep iron skillet. Initially this should be stirred over very low heat, but not much attention is required once ingredients begin to cook. The pan may be pushed to the back of the stove and the contents left to stay warm until ready to serve.

1½ pound steak

3 teaspoons olive oil

2 cloves garlic, minced

½ onion, chopped

4 stalks celery, chopped

2 16-ounce cans of black beans or small kidney beans

2½ cups water

2 teaspoons salt

½ teaspoon pepper

½ cup ketchup

Hot pepper sauce, to taste

Cut steak into ½-inch cubes. Heat olive oil in large skillet.

Add steak to skillet and cook until browned.

Push against side of pan and add garlic, onion, and celery. Sauté 2–3 minutes.

Mix in remaining ingredients and simmer for ½ hour.

Serve with large plate of toast or rice.

# *Beef Stew*

6–8 servings

Every so often, the cookstove in Tasha's house had a pot of stew simmering toward the back beside the copper double boiler. Tasha kept the double boiler full of water with the top on and used it to keep her meals warm or thaw the occasional fledgling waylaid by circumstance. One of the most famous birds resuscitated in this manner was Chickahominy, a bearded Belgium bantam whose mother abandoned him beneath an outbuilding. Tasha rolled the unresponsive orphan out with a hoe one late cold morning and resuscitated him. He lived happily and in great comfort for many years after. He never could stand the cold, however, and was inclined to pass out if exposed to temperatures approaching freezing. He was partial to beef stew.

| | |
|---|---|
| 2 pounds beef | 2 cups peeled and diced potatoes |
| Flour to coat meat | 1 cup peeled and diced turnips |
| Salt and pepper | 2 cups peeled and diced carrots |
| 1 tablespoon butter | ½ cup peeled and diced parsnips |
| 1 quart water | 2 beef bouillon cubes |
| 4 cloves garlic, minced | ½ teaspoon thyme |
| ½ cup chopped yellow onion | ½ teaspoon parsley |
| 1 green pepper, diced | 2 bay leaves |
| 1 cup sliced celery | 1 tablespoon flour |

Cut beef into cubes and coat in flour seasoned with salt and pepper. Sauté in butter. Add water and simmer 2 hours. Add remaining ingredients. Cover and simmer until vegetables are cooked. Add water when needed.

# Broccoli

## 4 servings

Tasha frequently ate broccoli. She boiled it until it was soft, then added salt and butter. She avoided the stems. Her only detraction from it was that she knew of no other food that got cold so quickly once removed from the pot. During winter she kept boxes of frozen broccoli in her freezer. Later in the summer she picked broccoli from her garden. She liked the little side shoots that sprouted after the main head was picked. Rabbits often ate the broccoli starts Tasha put out in the spring. At night she covered the little plants with a basket, which helped a great deal, and as the plants matured the rabbits moved on to other vegetables.

1 pound broccoli

Salt

Butter

Cut broccoli florets from stem.

Add to plenty of boiling water.

Boil uncovered with a little salt, 4–5 minutes, until soft.

Drain right away, add a teaspoon or two of butter, and shake the pot around a few times to cover broccoli. Serve immediately.

# Carrot Soup

### 4–6 servings

This receipt easily accommodates extra carrots or a variation of most other ingredients. If there are a lot of carrots on hand you could put in 2 pounds, for example. Tasha kept a close eye on the rows of carrots in the vegetable garden, and thinned them often. Small carrots are very good cooked whole or unpeeled, and frequent thinning allows storage carrots more room to grow and more water into the soil. Tasha actively managed her vegetable garden and continually harvested to keep production up. Many vegetable plants such as peas, zucchini, and chard stop growing once they mature, and frequent harvesting to keep them growing yields more food in the long run.

| | |
|---|---|
| 1 cup chopped onion | 1 tomato, chopped |
| 1 tablespoon minced fresh ginger | 3–4 cups chicken or vegetable stock |
| 1 clove garlic, minced | 2 tablespoons lemon juice |
| 4 tablespoons butter | Salt and pepper, to taste |
| 1 pound carrots, chopped | |

Sauté onion, ginger, and garlic in butter. Add carrots, tomato, and chicken or vegetable stock, and bring to boil.

Reduce heat, cover, and simmer 15 minutes or until carrots are soft.

Let soup cool a little, then pour in blender and puree. Add lemon juice, and salt and pepper to taste.

Garnish with sour cream or grated carrot.

The Tasha Tudor Family Cookbook

# Cauliflower with Cheese Sauce

4 servings

When a successful crop of cauliflower showed up in the vegetable garden, Tasha made this dish. Success depends on setting the plants out really early so they mature before turning bitter from summer temperatures. Blanch the heads a week before picking by partially breaking three or four exterior leaves and tucking the ends on each head's opposite side. The excellent texture of cauliflower is lost when the heads begin to blossom, so it is important to pick or buy before the buds release, usually around 6 inches across.

| | |
|---|---|
| 1 head cauliflower | 2 cups milk |
| 4 tablespoons butter | ¼–½ cup shredded cheddar cheese |
| ¼ cup all-purpose flour | ¼ cup crushed crackers |

Steam a whole cauliflower head, 15–20 minutes or until tender.

While cauliflower is cooking, make cream sauce. Melt butter in skillet over medium-low heat.

Whisk in flour and stir for 2 minutes. Add milk and cheese, stirring frequently until mixture thickens, 6–8 minutes.

Place cauliflower stem side down in baking dish. Pour cream sauce over top and sprinkle crushed crackers over all.

Bake for 15 minutes at 350°F.

# Chicken or Beef Pie

6 servings

The chicken and beef pies Tasha baked had a heavy, hearty pastry, with a solid filling of chunks of beef or chicken, potato, carrot, and onions, cooked in a deep pie dish.

PIE CRUST:

2 cups sifted all-purpose flour

1 teaspoon salt

⅔ cup plus 2 tablespoons shortening

¼ cup ice water

CREAM SAUCE:

4 tablespoons butter

¼ cup flour

2 cups milk

FILLING:

2 pounds cooked chicken, or 2 pounds cooked beef

2 carrots, chopped and cooked

4 potatoes, peeled, chopped, and cooked

½ onion, diced and sautéed

½ cup peas

Salt, to taste

To make the pie crust, mix flour and salt. Dump in shortening and cut until size of peas. Sprinkle with water. Gather together. Press into ball. Divide in half. Cook dough 10 minutes at 475°F.

To make the cream sauce, melt butter in skillet over medium-low heat. Whisk in flour and stir for 2 minutes. Add milk, simmer, and stir frequently until mixture thickens, 6–8 minutes.

Add filling ingredients to the partially cooked crust, add cream sauce, top with remaining crust, and bake ½ hour or until top crust is brown.

# Chicken Noodle Soup

## 4–6 servings

Tasha made many variations of chicken soup. They all start out with stock from a chicken roasted and enjoyed the day before and the remaining meat and bones simmered in water with carrots, onion, garlic, bay leaves, and a teaspoon each of chopped tarragon, thyme, and parsley, and some basil. Tasha made a light chicken soup during summer and a more filling version for colder months. This is one of her basic winter chicken soup receipts.

6 cups chicken stock

2 cups egg noodles

¼ cup all-purpose flour

¾ cup water

½ cup heavy cream

2 cups cooked, chopped chicken

Salt and pepper, to taste

Fresh parsley to garnish

Bring stock to boil, add egg noodles, and cook 8 minutes.

In separate bowl, mix flour and water into a paste and add to stock. Bring back to boil for 2 minutes.

Stir in cream and chopped chicken.

Add salt and pepper to taste and garnish with fresh parsley.

# Fish and Potato

## Makes 8–10 1½-inch patties

Every week or two, swordfish, salmon, or cod was on the menu. For special occasions, Tasha cooked fish in seashells in the oven with crumbled Ritz Crackers on top, but otherwise just used a glass baking dish. Leftover fish returned for lunch the next day, often mixed with potatoes and with a side dish of asparagus, broccoli, or peas. Minou, the one-eyed cat, especially looked forward to fish, and would purr hopefully as the time for supper approached. Tasha always gave her a little, up on a counter where the dogs could not reach.

1 cup mashed potatoes

1 cup cooked fish

½ tablespoon butter

1 egg

¼ teaspoon salt

⅛ teaspoon pepper

3 tablespoons chopped dill

In large bowl, mix all ingredients.

Form into small, flat ¼–½-inch cakes.

Place gently in oiled skillet and cook 10–12 minutes, flipping once, until browned on both sides.

Serve with ketchup and vegetables.

# Lentil Soup

### About 6 servings

This is an old and satisfying receipt. Adjustments of herbs and salt can be made to meet most anyone's taste. Tasha stored dried beans and lentils on a top shelf in a series of graduated glass jars with metal press-on lids.

4 tablespoons olive oil

2 stalks celery, chopped

1 onion, chopped

4 carrots, chopped

1 teaspoon basil

1 teaspoon dried oregano

4 cloves garlic, minced

2 bay leaves

8 cups chicken stock, or 8 cups water

2 tomatoes, diced, or 1 can stewed tomatoes

2 cups uncooked lentils

2 cups chopped fresh spinach

1 tablespoon balsamic vinegar

Salt and pepper, to taste

Heat oil in large pot. Add celery, onion, and carrot. Stir in basil, oregano, garlic, and bay leaves.

Add chicken stock or water, tomato, and lentils. Bring to boil, then simmer an hour or so. Top each serving with fresh spinach tossed in balsamic vinegar. Add salt and pepper to taste.

This soup tends to thicken over time and you may want to add extra liquid. Sausage or beef makes a good addition.

# Macaroni and Cheese

## 4–6 servings

Anot infrequent presence at lunch or supper, this dish is beloved by the many people who have stopped by Tasha's house over the years and stayed to eat. The receipt doubles easily. Often Tasha made a dish of macaroni and cheese the day before she anticipated guests, but instead of baking, refrigerated it. An hour before lunch the next day she topped it with crackers and baked it. At times she made macaroni and cheese in several smaller bowls to serve individually.

6 cups water

2 cups elbow macaroni

5 tablespoons butter

¼ cup all-purpose flour

2 cups milk

4 ounces sharp cheddar cheese, cubed

4 ounces Velveeta, cubed

Salt and pepper, to taste

1 crushed package of Ritz Crackers

To a pot of boiling water, add macaroni and cook until tender. Preheat oven to 350°F.

Meanwhile, melt butter in an 8-inch saucepan on medium-low heat. Add flour and stir until smooth.

Add milk and cheese. Stir frequently until mixture begins to thicken. Add salt and pepper to taste. Stir in drained macaroni. Top with crushed crackers and bake 25 minutes or until browned.

Occasionally, Tasha sprinkled Parmesan cheese on the cracker topping prior to baking, or stirred finely chopped garlic into the sauce. She crushed the crackers in the wax paper sleeve they came in by pressing down on them with a rolling pin.

# Meatballs

## 6 servings, 18 1½–inch balls

This receipt goes well with potatoes, rice, pasta, and bread. The uncooked meatballs remain good frozen for two to three months, should you want to make a large batch up but cook only a few. This original receipt does not call for onions, but is receptive to additional ingredients. A good meat loaf can be made from these ingredients, too, minus the stock. Tasha seemed to make this receipt during the days leading up to Christmas.

Meatballs overmixed during preparation will be tough. Overcooked meatballs will be dry.

24 ounces turkey burger, or 12 ounces turkey burger and 12 ounces hamburger

1 cup quick rolled oats

½ cup ketchup

2 eggs

1 teaspoon ground thyme

1 teaspoon salt

¼ cup grated Parmesan

2 tablespoons olive oil

2–3 cups beef stock

Mix all ingredients except olive oil and beef stock until just evenly combined. Form into 1-inch balls.

Heat 2 tablespoons olive oil in 10-inch or larger skillet. Add meatballs, then add stock.

Cook to 160°F.

# Rice and Tomato

4 servings

This is a dish Tasha ate frequently in the 1930s. She made it on a regular basis in later decades as well, generally during late summer when a lot of tomatoes were ripe, or when she was feeling especially frugal. "It's all we ate during the summer back then," she would say, not complaining, but remembering. During the Great Depression, a large and productive vegetable garden was the primary source of food for many families. Tasha was in her late teens and early twenties during that period of history, and had a great many memories from that time. She was more likely to share them during this meal. It is very good.

2 cups water

½ teaspoon salt

1 teaspoon butter

1 cup long-grain white rice

Stewed tomatoes, canned or fresh (about 2 cups, or 2 tomatoes)

Bring water to boil. Add salt and butter.

Stir in rice, cover with tight-fitting lid, and simmer 20 minutes. Only a trickle of steam should escape lid. If a lot does, burner is too high. Don't lift lid.

The omission of salt and/or butter won't affect cooking.

Fluff rice with fork, place on dish, and add stewed tomatoes. Fresh basil, pepper, and cheddar cheese may also be added.

Tasha invariably removed the skin from fresh tomatoes by dipping them whole in boiling water a half minute, then peeling the skin off with a knife.

# Rice, Carrots, and Chicken

### 4–5 servings

Tasha made this dish more often when late summer arrived and the vegetable garden was at peak production. She added side dishes of peas, broccoli, beets, or string beans. The rice and carrots cooked together complement one another in a way that isn't achieved if cooked separately.

| | |
|---|---|
| 2¼ cups water | 4 carrots |
| 1 teaspoon salt | 1 cup white rice |
| 2 tablespoons butter | 2 cups cooked, diced chicken |

Bring water to boil. Add salt and 1 tablespoon butter.

Stir in carrots and rice, cover with tight-fitting lid, and simmer 20 minutes. Only a trickle of steam should escape lid. If a lot does, burner is too high. Don't lift lid until rice is done.

Add chicken and remaining butter.

# Roast Beef and Cream Sauce

## 2 servings

Tasha bought roast beef to celebrate New Year's. It was often a large roast and the leftovers were looked forward to as much as the roast itself. The size of the roast diminished each day as it was used in the dinners and suppers that followed the main event. One memorable presentation involved a thick slice of toasted wheat bread, topped with a blend of cream sauce and chopped-up roast beef with broccoli on the side.

| | |
|---|---|
| 4 tablespoons butter | Bread |
| ¼ cup flour | Roast beef |
| 2 cups milk | |

Melt butter in skillet over medium-low heat. Whisk in flour and stir for 2 minutes.

Add milk and simmer, stirring frequently until mixture thickens, 6–8 minutes.

Toast thick slice of bread and put on plate.

Add chopped-up roast beef and cream sauce to top of toast.

# Roast Chicken

## 4 servings

Aroasted chicken may be served hot with a main meal, later as chicken sandwiches or chicken salad, and finally as chicken soup. Little remains by then. Tasha burned the bones in the woodstove and later spread the ash on the garden to raise the pH. For traditional meals such as Christmas and Thanksgiving, Tasha used a reflector oven to roast a turkey. For special occasions involving a smaller number of dinner guests, she roasted an appropriate-size fowl. She emphasized the importance of using fresh herbs in baking, and a common sight around mealtime was Tasha going to or from the herb garden with a small basket and a very long pair of scissors.

1 roasting chicken, 6 pounds

Salt

Pepper

Butter or cold bacon drippings

4 cloves garlic, peeled

1 large onion, peeled

4 fresh bay leaves

Fresh tarragon

Fresh sage

Preheat oven to 350°F.

Wash and dry chicken, and place in roasting pan. Put salt and pepper on chicken. Rub with butter or bacon drippings.

Cut a slot beside each drumstick and put 1 clove of garlic in each.

Stuff chicken with onion, bay leaves, tarragon, sage, and remaining garlic.

Truss chicken, and bake 2 hours or until 160°F. Baste often.

The Tasha Tudor Family Cookbook

# Salmon

## 2–3 servings

Tasha ate fish about once a week, usually the day of the week the market brought them in. She was particular about fresh fish, and if the selection behind the counter didn't appeal to her she'd ask if something better was out back. Often there was. Tasha paired roasted salmon with hard-boiled eggs and vegetables, or thinly sliced potatoes cooked in olive oil and rosemary.

1 tablespoon butter

1 tablespoon olive oil

¼ teaspoon salt

12-ounce salmon fillet

Preheat oven to 500°F.

In small pan, heat butter, olive oil, and salt. Spoon half into baking dish and add salmon.

Pour rest of butter, olive oil, and salt across top of fish.

Roast for 5 minutes. Turn fish over and roast 5 more minutes or until done, about 145°F or until flesh is opaque and easily separates with fork.

Serve with parsley butter (page 109).

# Split Pea Soup

## 4–6 servings

There are enough soup receipts in Tasha's collection to make an entire cookbook. Many derived from the momentum that comes from buying and using basic ingredients and not throwing food away. Soups are a good way to use up odds and ends in the refrigerator, and make them taste good, too. Peas were one of Tasha's favorite vegetables, particularly fresh peas. In summer she gathered a half bushel of her preferred variety, Thomas Laxton, from the vegetable garden and shelled them in a yellow ware bowl while she sat in her rocking chair on the front porch. The bowl sat on the table to her right, and the table usually had on a red tablecloth with a vase of flowers in the back corner. During hot weather this is where she had regular tea. She enjoyed hot, muggy weather.

2 cups split green peas

2 quarts cold water

1 cup chopped yellow onions

3 carrots, chopped

3 stalks celery with leaves, chopped

1 meaty ham bone

8 ounces diced ham

Salt and pepper, to taste

After washing and sorting peas, place in water, cover, and bring to boil. Simmer 2 minutes, remove from heat, and let stand 1 hour.

Add vegetables, bring back up to a boil, then return to a simmer and cover 2½ hours. Add ham bone halfway through cooking time.

Once peas are soft, remove ham bone, cool soup, and strain through colander. Add diced ham to each serving and season with salt and pepper.

# Christmas Turkey

## 1 pound of turkey per person

Tasha kept the fireplace going all winter, so every morning there were coals on the hearth. She put the turkey in the tin kitchen early on Christmas, and by the time everyone gathered for dinner the house smelled of mashed potatoes, gravy, sugar cookies, fresh bread, and roast turkey. The strings of balsam branches around the doorway and the wreath with the red bow smelled wonderful, candlelight gleamed in the copperware over the cookstove, corgis ran about barking, and the frequent ring of the telephone from acquaintances calling to say Merry Christmas was part of the scene. The most memorable sound, though, was the click of the entry door latch, because as soon as you put your hand on it, the door opened into this world. It would be hard to overstate Tasha's enthusiasm and energy for this time of year, and it was always wonderful to celebrate Christmas with her in her home.

Turkey                                    Pepper

Salt                                       Bacon drippings

It takes a steady bed of coals with a fire in the background and about 5–7 hours, depending on size, to roast the turkey. Many old reflector ovens have long ago lost their shine and are but a dull, dark gray. It takes longer to cook a turkey on one of those than in a new one.

To roast a turkey in a tin kitchen or reflector oven:

Rub turkey with salt, pepper, and bacon drippings. Stuff bird, secure firmly on spit, place tin kitchen before fire, and turn every 20 minutes. Baste frequently with drippings. Check for doneness with thermometer as roasting nears completion.

# Thin Bread Sandwiches

### 1 sandwich per serving

Thin bread sandwiches were a quintessential feature in Tasha's household. She sliced bread thin to make picnic sandwiches and tea sandwiches alike. She used either mayonnaise—always Hellmann's—or butter on those sandwiches that required it. Sometimes a thin slice of bread is apt to break while being made into a sandwich, so Tasha would butter the bread before cutting a slice from the loaf.

Below are a few of the more frequent combinations:

Cucumber and butter

Chicken with herbs

Peanut butter and marshmallow fluff

Cream cheese and jam, raspberry or strawberry

Cream cheese and chives

Ham spread and butter

# *Tomato Soup*

**6 servings**

Tasha's vegetable garden always had tomato plants. They did very well, but when first set out were vulnerable to cutworms. To thwart them, she wrapped a spacious collar of newspaper around the tomato stem so that it extended an inch or so below the soil once planted, and an inch above.

TOMATO SOUP:

2 cups canned or fresh tomatoes

½ cup chopped celery

½ cup chopped onion

2 teaspoons brown sugar

SAUCE:

½ onion

4 cloves

6 tablespoons butter

Salt and pepper, to taste

3 cups milk

⅔ cup tomato paste

1 beef bouillon cube dissolved in a cup
 of boiling water

1 cup hot water

Crumbled-up sweet basil leaf or chopped fresh one

To make the soup, combine all ingredients, simmer for 20 minutes, and put through sieve. Set aside.

To make the sauce, take ½ onion and stick 4 cloves in it.

Melt butter in heavy pan and add salt and pepper. Add milk slowly to keep from lumping. Add onion and boil 5 minutes. Remove onion.

Add tomato paste, beef bouillon cube, hot water, and sweet basil leaf. Season to taste with salt and pepper. You may want to add more tomato paste if flavor isn't strong enough. Heat thoroughly in double boiler before serving. Blend if soup curdles. Tasha used Hunt's tomato paste.

# Winter Squash Soup

### 6–8 servings

Blue Hubbard squash tends to make the most flavorful soup, but all winter squash such as butternut or acorn work well, and butternut is the easiest to work with. When cured in a warm, airy location for a couple of weeks and then stored in a cool, dry, dark spot, winter squash last many months. Fully mature squash have less moisture content, which makes for better soup and better storage. In the old days, bedrooms were usually unheated, and the space beneath a four-poster provided ideal storage conditions. A lot of root cellars are too damp to store squash.

| | |
|---|---|
| 2-pound squash | 4 cups vegetable or chicken stock |
| ½ cup mild yellow onion or leeks, chopped | 1 teaspoon salt |
| 2 tablespoons butter | 3 teaspoons fresh minced ginger |

Preheat oven to 400°F.

Cut squash in half lengthwise. Place cut side down on oiled sheet or baking dish in oven for an hour or until soft.

Meanwhile, in a large soup pot, sauté onion or leeks in butter.

When squash is cool, remove pulp and add to sautéed onion or leeks.

Add vegetable or chicken stock, salt, and ginger.

Simmer and stir 15–20 minutes. Whisk vigorously for a smooth soup.

# Fruits and Salads

# Bean Salad

6–8 servings

Whenever Tasha came across a receipt that appealed to her, she adapted it to her tastes and copied it into her cookbook. She generally ate what was in season, and tried to grow as many fruits and vegetables as she could. This receipt was added to her collection in the 1960s. It was a menu item during summer when she set the table on the front porch, right around the time the roses were in bloom.

1 16-ounce can kidney beans

1½ cups fresh chopped green beans

1 16-ounce can yellow wax beans

1 16-ounce can lima beans

1 4-ounce jar pimientos

1 small red onion, diced

1 cup vinegar

½ cup olive oil

1 teaspoon salt

½ teaspoon celery salt

½ cup sugar

Drain kidney beans, green beans, wax beans, lima beans, pimientos, and onion. Put in large bowl.

Bring vinegar, oil, salt, celery salt, and sugar to boil. Cool and pour over beans. Mix well.

Leave in refrigerator overnight. This receipt tastes better 1 and 2 days later than when just made.

# Carrot Salad

2 servings

Tasha frequently employed a meat grinder to make leftover ham, chicken, and turkey into croquettes. The grinder was also very useful for grinding root vegetables such as carrots, and was often employed to make the following receipt. This grinder is still around and just as effective and useful as it was eighty years ago.

6 carrots, peeled

¼ cup raisins

1 tablespoon lemon juice

¼ teaspoon salt

2–4 tablespoons mayonnaise

Grind carrots, then add raisins, lemon juice, and salt.

Mix in mayonnaise and serve.

# Kale Salad

## 2 servings

Tasha planted kale twice, early in spring and again in midsummer. The midsummer crop was intended to last well into the winter, but every now and then a tree fell on the garden fence and moments later, it seemed, deer had eaten a twenty-foot row of kale down to the stems. Tasha didn't like that, but such an incident prompted her to sympathize with farmers whose livelihood depended on the success of a crop.

Kale

Apples, chopped

Dried cranberries

Walnuts

Grated carrots

DRESSING:

1 tablespoon lemon juice

1 tablespoon olive oil

Dash of salt

Dash of chili powder

A few dashes of balsamic vinegar

Wash and dry kale. Remove stems, chop finely, then massage to break down fibers. Add desired amount of apples, cranberries, walnuts, and carrots.

To make the dressing, combine all ingredients in a mason jar and shake until mixed. Pour desired amount over salad.

Lasts a couple days covered with damp paper towel in refrigerator.

# Orange and Banana

## 2 servings

This simple dish is a traditional dessert year-round. Bananas and oranges are often the first fruit in a fruit salad bowl to disappear, so why not just skip the other fruits? As the seasons pass, the availability of good oranges fluctuates. If an orange feels heavy in the hand, it is a better orange than one of the same size that feels lighter. A ripe orange has no soft spots and is firm with a smooth, thin skin. It is best if the banana in this receipt has brown ripening spots and the stem is beginning to wilt and soften. At this ripeness bananas are sweet, less starchy, and easier to digest.

2 ripe bananas, peeled and sliced

2 oranges, peeled

Separate orange sections and cut up. Stir banana and orange together.

Serve immediately, either plain or with whipped cream.

# Pear and Arugula Salad

## 4 servings

Tasha got most of her pears from a large Bartlett pear tree below and to the west of her house. She planted it when she came to live in Vermont in the 1960s. It bore quantities of pears in late summer and early autumn. When a pear was required she walked out the front door, off the porch, past the campanula, and down the grassy slope to the tree. As the first frost neared the last of the pears were picked and stored in baskets in the dairy.

| | |
|---|---|
| 1 tablespoon maple syrup | 2 tablespoons olive oil |
| 1 teaspoon vinegar | 8 cups fresh arugula |
| 1 teaspoon stone-ground mustard | 1 pear, unpeeled, sliced thin |
| ¼ teaspoon salt | ½ cup extra-sharp cheddar cheese |

Make a vinaigrette by whisking together maple syrup, vinegar, mustard, and salt, while slowly adding oil.

Place arugula on salad plates and add slices of pear and cheese.

Add desired amount of vinaigrette.

# Accompaniments

# Cream Sauce

This sauce is essential for creaming vegetables and as a base for macaroni and cheese. It is smooth, mild, and easily made. It is quickly thinned if cooked too thick, but not easily thickened if cooked too thin. How much cream sauce to add to a dish is subject to taste, as is the amount of salt, pepper, or herbs. However, even small amounts of flavor have a large impact.

4 tablespoons butter

¼ cup flour

2 cups milk

¼ teaspoon salt

Melt butter in skillet over medium-low heat. Whisk in flour and stir for 2 minutes. Add milk, simmer, and stir frequently until mixture thickens, about 6–8 minutes. Add salt and stir.

# Ham Spread

Tasha received plenty of packages in the mail—some she ordered, others friends and acquaintances sent. But when reasonably possible Tasha preferred to drive to the business that provided the merchandise she wished to buy, sometimes just to check it out to see what kind of operation it was, particularly if she was unfamiliar with the company but interested in what it sold. Each year, a month or so before Christmas, she made a trip to northern Vermont to acquire an assortment of particularly good baked hams. Some she gave away, others she kept for special occasions in the near future. One of the most frequent and enduring receipts she made was ham spread. She applied it to the top of macaroni and cheese and used it for a sandwich filling, for a cracker spread, and for flavoring rice or potato dishes. She prepared it with one of the few modern conveniences in her kitchen, a Cuisinart. A blender will work as well.

6 ounces precooked ham, cubed

3 ounces sharp cheddar cheese

1 or 2 cloves garlic, peeled

Process ingredients well in Cuisinart. If using in sandwiches, add 1 tablespoon mayonnaise before processing.

Keeps well for up to a week if sealed and refrigerated.

# *Parsley Butter*

Tasha usually served this with roast salmon. She was more likely to make parsley butter during the spring and summer when her herb garden flourished and fresh parsley and dill were close at hand. She grew several small citrus trees in her greenhouse, and was especially delighted when a crop of lemons ripened, usually not more than half a dozen. This amount was far too small to meet her needs, however, and she bought the vast majority of limes and lemons she required from the grocery store.

¼ cup butter, at room temperature

½ tablespoon fresh parsley, chopped, plus additional sprigs for garnish

½ teaspoon salt

⅛ teaspoon pepper

2½ teaspoons lemon juice

1 teaspoon fresh dill, chopped

Beat the butter until soft and smooth. Add the chopped parsley, salt, and pepper. Slowly stir in lemon juice. Add fresh dill. Form the butter into a mound with a small bowl or butter mold and place on a serving dish, adorned with fresh parsley sprigs.

# Pastry

## Makes 2 9–inch pie crusts

This is the pastry Tasha used for apple pie, pumpkin pie, blueberry pie, and cherry pie, among others. She always rolled it out on the marble countertop and into the desired shape with several quick, sweeping motions. The marble kept the dough cool and butter from melting. She usually used a wooden rolling pin, though she did have one made of marble on a lower shelf in the kitchen.

2½ cups all-purpose flour, sifted

1 teaspoon salt

⅔ cup plus 2 tablespoons shortening

¼ cup iced water

Mix flour and salt. Dump in shortening and cut until size of peas. Sprinkle with water. Gather together and press into ball. Divide in half and gently flatten into two discs. Cover and refrigerate for at least ½ hour. On a lightly floured surface roll the dough from the center out. Work the dough as little as possible. Instead of pushing down on the rolling pin, lean into it. Transfer dough by draping it around the rolling pin. Press dough into entire bottom of the pie plate and then up along sides. Use scissors to trim excess edges.

# Stuffing

Tasha liked Pepperidge Farm's products. The Pepperidge Farm bakery was started in 1937 in Fairfield, Connecticut, by a housewife and mother of three young children, the general time and area Tasha was starting out as a housewife and mother. This receipt is an instance where she added her own ingredients to another receipt. She made this stuffing for turkeys roasted during the holidays.

2½ cups chicken stock

½ cup butter

16-ounce package Pepperidge Farm herb-seasoned stuffing

1 large onion, finely chopped

4 ribs celery, chopped

6 cloves garlic, minced

1 cup fresh mixed herbs, such as parsley, thyme, savory, sage, and marjoram

In saucepan over low heat, bring chicken stock and butter to boil. Remove from heat. Place stuffing and remaining ingredients in mixing bowl. Pour stock and butter over all and toss lightly to mix. When roasting a turkey, place stuffing in bird so it remains loose, and not packed. The bird and stuffing need to be cooked to 165°F. Tasha roasted turkeys in a tin kitchen in front of the fireplace, which took between 4 and 6 hours for a 20-pound turkey.

# Desserts

# Apple Pie

## 8 servings

During the 1920s, Tasha participated in outdoor tea parties beneath an old apple tree in Connecticut. Many decades later, she tried to get a cutting from that tree to plant in her garden in Vermont. Upon inquiry she learned the tree was gone, and had been gone since the hurricane of 1938. Nevertheless, she remembered the characteristics of the apples the tree bore and in time discovered the cultivar, and soon thereafter obtained a sapling. She planted it below and southwest of her front porch. It stands on the edge of the lawn beside the expanse of daffodils that in early spring turn the flattened winter grass into a sea of fragrant yellow. This tree now produces late summer apples excellent for pies.

Pastry for 2 9-inch pie crusts (page 118)

3 pounds apples (6–8 apples)

1 teaspoon cinnamon

½ cup sugar

⅛ teaspoon salt

Preheat oven to 475°F. Prepare pastry as described on page 110. Bake 10 minutes before adding filling. Reduce oven temperature to 425°F.

Peel and core apples and slice ¼ inch thick. Mix in cinnamon, sugar, and salt and let sit about 10 minutes.

Pour into pie crust and press down on apples with a spoon or hand to settle the mixture. Add top crust and slash several times with knife.

Bake for 20 minutes, then lower oven to 350°F and bake for 30 minutes.

Tasha tried not to overbake apple pies. If the sliced apples retain some texture, the pie seems to taste even better.

# Applesauce

## 4 servings

There are a half dozen apple trees in Tasha's garden that take turns producing apples from late summer through fall. The early apples tend to keep poorly, while those that ripen right up to frost last about half a year. Most make excellent applesauce, particularly when two or three varieties are combined. Whenever a bumper crop came along, Tasha made apple pies, applesauce cake, apple crisp, apple butter, apple cobblers, and applesauce. She generally served the applesauce as a side dish or dessert, still warm from the stove, and was always delighted when guests asked what she put in her applesauce to make it so good.

4 large apples

Water

Wash, peel, core, and cut apples. Tasha often used half Empire apples and half Cortland. Place in pot along with ½ cup of water, or a little more if apples are not fresh.

Cover, and simmer on low. Stir often with wooden spoon for 20 minutes or until apples are soft and dissolved, but not overcooked.

For chunky applesauce, no more steps are necessary. Once removed from heat, however, Tasha would quickly stir the applesauce for up to a minute, making a smoother texture. For an even smoother applesauce, work through a coarse sieve.

# Applesauce Cake

## 10 servings

Tasha collected apples in a green-ash-splint basket before they fell and stored them on the counter beside the bread box, where over the next few days she made them into applesauce or pies. She baked cookies or a cake each day to have ready for afternoon tea and visitors. If guests arrived early they helped prepare tea, carried in an armload of firewood, put new candles in the candleholders, or moved weed piles to the compost, depending on the season. Sometimes Tasha frosted the applesauce cake, other times she didn't.

CAKE:

¾ cup sugar

1 egg

8 tablespoons butter, soft

1½ cups all-purpose flour

¾ teaspoon baking soda

FROSTING:

1 cup brown sugar

½ cup cream

½ teaspoon salt

1 teaspoon cinnamon

½ teaspoon ground cloves

1 cup applesauce, unsweetened

1 tablespoon butter

½ teaspoon vanilla

Preheat oven to 350°F.

First make the cake. In large mixing bowl, beat together sugar, egg, and butter. Add flour, baking soda, salt, cinnamon, cloves, and applesauce. Mix until just combined.

Bake in greased 8x8-inch pan 25–30 minutes or until a fork or toothpick inserted in center comes out clean.

While the cake is baking, make the frosting. Bring brown sugar and cream to a simmer and cook to 235°F. Turn burner off and cool until about 100°F. Add butter and vanilla. Beat until frosting thickens and frost cake right away.

The Tasha Tudor Family Cookbook

# Baked Apples

## 10–12 servings

Good cooking apples are crisp, tart, and inclined to store well. Jonagold and Winesap are two varieties to consider. However, Tasha cooked with what apples were at hand. Baked apples were quite common during winter nights around the fire. They were cored, filled with brown sugar and raisins, and baked 10–12 minutes in a pan. The brown sugar melts, saturates the apples, and turns to syrup. She kept a crank-operated apple peeler/corer in the hen pantry. When she canned large quantities of applesauce or baked a lot of pies, she clamped it to the edge of the kitchen counter and went to work. Many decades ago baked apples were more often peeled and cut rather than baked whole, but the method below is how Tasha went about it.

10–12 apples

1½ cups brown sugar

¾ cup raisins

1 teaspoon nutmeg

1 teaspoon cinnamon

Preheat oven to 350°F.

Wash and core 10–12 apples. Combine brown sugar, raisins, nutmeg, and cinnamon. Divide mixture and fill apples.

Place apples in baking dish with ¼ inch or more cold water in the bottom and bake, covered, 30–50 minutes or until apples are soft but have not begun to crumble and turn into applesauce.

Apples that have been sitting around a while cook faster than fresh apples, so cooking time varies. By the time the apples have baked, the water and some of the sugar from the apples will have turned to syrup.

Serve with heavy cream poured over the baked apple.

# Brownies

### Makes 2 dozen 2×2-inch brownies

Tasha spent many of the days between late spring and early autumn in her garden. During the cold and short days of winter she worked on writing or illustrating. She sat at the end of her art table with the north window on her left and the fireplace on her right. Invariably, there was some sort of sweet close by. This is Tasha's favorite brownie receipt, one that she usually made during early winter months just after daylight saving time ended and it became dark around four in the afternoon. She especially enjoyed the frosting.

BROWNIES:

| | |
|---|---|
| 1 cup plus 2 tablespoons butter | 2 cups sugar |
| ¾ cup baking cocoa | 1½ cups all-purpose flour |
| 4 eggs | 1 teaspoon salt |
| 1 teaspoon vanilla | 1 teaspoon baking powder |

FROSTING:

| | |
|---|---|
| 6 tablespoons butter, melted | 1 teaspoon vanilla |
| 2⅔ cups confectioners' sugar | ⅓ cup milk |
| ½ cup baking cocoa | |

Preheat oven to 350°F.

To make the brownies, heat butter until just melted and place in bottom of mixing bowl. Add cocoa, eggs, vanilla, then remaining ingredients. Mix well.

Bake in 9 × 13-inch pan for about 25 minutes, or until fork comes out of center clean. Avoid overbaking. Cool in pan or on rack.

To make the frosting, melt butter, add remaining ingredients, and mix thoroughly. Spread over brownies and cut into bars.

The Tasha Tudor Family Cookbook

# Charlotte Cake

## 12 servings

If there was only one way to make a chocolate cake, this would be it. Ned Hills's sister Charlotte Brown introduced this receipt to the family in the 1950s. Tasha called this cake a "stunner," and it is. Baked in a 9 × 15-inch pan and frosted with ½ inch white vanilla frosting made with butter, cream, and vanilla, the cake is rich, moist, and irresistible. This cake falls very easily and the oven door should remain shut until nearly the end of baking.

CAKE:

2 cups sugar

¾ cup corn oil

1 egg

4 teaspoons baking soda

2½ cups all-purpose flour

⅔ cup cocoa

¾ teaspoon salt

2 cups buttermilk

FROSTING:

¼ pound soft butter

2 pounds powdered sugar

Pinch of salt

1 tablespoon vanilla

Enough cream for spreading easily, ½ cup or so

Preheat oven to 350°F.

To make the cake, mix together sugar and oil. Add egg and beat well. Add dry ingredients alternating with buttermilk. Pour into greased and floured pan. Bake for about ½ hour.

To make the frosting, in a large mixing bowl, combine butter, sugar, and salt. Beat thoroughly for 1 minute with large spoon. Add vanilla and beat for 1 more minute. Add cream a little at a time, beating until frosting reaches the desired consistency. Cake should be cool prior to frosting.

# Chocolate Chip Cookies

## Makes 3 dozen 2½–inch cookies

Tasha referred to the chocolate chips in chocolate chip cookies as chocolate beans, and one of the distinguishing features of her chocolate chip cookies was the abundance of chocolate beans she incorporated in the batter. She had a distinct ingredient assembly and mixing method that gave her chocolate chip cookies an excellent taste and texture. First, the butter must be so soft that it's nearly melted. Second, the ingredients should be mixed as little as possible, just enough so they cannot be distinguished from one another. The cookies should not be underbaked or overbaked. The edges should be just beginning to brown, and the sheen of batter just disappearing when removed from the oven. Immediately remove cookies from cookie sheet to a wire rack. This last process inevitably damages a few cookies, which provides a sample for the baker.

| | |
|---|---|
| ¾ cup light brown sugar | 2¼ cups all-purpose flour |
| ¾ cup sugar | 1 teaspoon salt |
| 1 cup unsalted butter, melted | 1 teaspoon baking soda |
| 1 teaspoon vanilla | 2–3 cups semisweet chocolate chips |
| 2 eggs | |

Preheat oven to 350°F.

Add brown sugar, sugar, butter, vanilla, eggs, flour, salt, and baking soda to a large mixing bowl. Mix ingredients until just combined, then add chocolate chips.

Drop rounded tablespoons of batter on cookie sheet, flatten slightly, and bake for 8–10 minutes or until conditions as described above are met.

Makes about 3 dozen and lasts up to a week in well-sealed container, or much longer when properly sealed in freezer. However, these cookies are at their best for 1–2 days.

### The Tasha Tudor Family Cookbook

# Chocolate Pudding

## 4 servings

Served warm with a scoop of vanilla ice cream, this dessert is a memorable experience. Tasha cooked puddings in double boilers. Hers has a lovely copper bottom and ceramic top. She stirred the pudding frequently, then constantly as it came to temperature, with a wooden spoon. As soon as it thickened she poured it into waiting bowls and refrigerated it. She liked the thick skin that formed as the pudding cooled, but for those who don't, it is easy to press plastic wrap directly to the pudding surface, which keeps the pudding soft. Kept this way it lasts two days in the refrigerator, but really should be eaten within a day. A tablespoon of heavy cream can take the place of ice cream. It does not take long to make chocolate pudding from scratch, and its equal in the form of a mix has yet to be invented.

½ cup sugar

⅓ cup unsweetened cocoa

⅓ cup water

2 cups whole milk

3 tablespoons cornstarch

1 teaspoon vanilla

Bring sugar, cocoa, and water to boil, stirring constantly. Add 1¾ cups milk.

In a small bowl, mix cornstarch and remaining milk.

Add to milk and cocoa mix and stir constantly until pudding begins to thicken. Lower heat and stir 1 minute. Mix in vanilla.

# Christmas Tree Gingerbread

## Makes 16–20 4-inch cookies

Many pages in Tasha's cookbooks have notes in the margins suggesting how to improve a receipt, or even a large X across the page to indicate she had found a version more to her liking. She primarily used this receipt for gingerbread houses and Christmas tree cookies. By the time Christmas was over, the gingerbread ornaments were pretty stale, and they wound up decorating trees outside, which the squirrels and birds appreciated.

GINGERBREAD:

| | |
|---|---|
| 1 cup butter | 1½ tablespoons ginger |
| 1 cup dark brown sugar | 2½ teaspoons salt |
| 3 eggs | 1½ teaspoons baking soda |
| 1½ cups molasses | 1 teaspoon cinnamon |
| 6 cups flour | |

FROSTING:

| | |
|---|---|
| 1½ cups sugar | 2 egg whites |
| ½ cup water | |

Preheat oven to 350°F.

To make the gingerbread, cream butter and add sugar, eggs, and molasses. Sift dry ingredients and combine with wet ingredients. Chill, roll out, and cut into shapes for the tree. Prick holes where the ribbons will be inserted to hang the shapes.

Bake on sheets until dry but not crisp, about 10–15 minutes, depending on thickness or until edges begin to darken.

To make the frosting, boil sugar and water to spin a fine thread. Beat egg whites. When syrup makes a fine thread, pour over egg whites and beat with an electric beater. Make a cone with wax paper and decorate your gingerbread cookies!

### The Tasha Tudor Family Cookbook

# Baked Custard

## 6 servings

Tasha kept chickens from her youth through old age. She had great affection for them. Not only did they supply eggs, but they were good subjects for illustrations. In winter when their outdoor run was covered in snow she provided greens, usually kale, and in the summer quantities of weeds from the garden. When the strengthening sun and longer days of spring arrived, so did a great many eggs. Such a surplus influenced Tasha's menu, and baked custard was a frequent dish. Most milk nowadays is pasteurized and it is therefore not necessary to scald it for this receipt.

4 cups milk

5 eggs, at room temperature

⅓ cup sugar

¼ teaspoon salt

1 teaspoon vanilla

Dash ground nutmeg

Preheat oven to 300°F.

Whip all ingredients together. Strain through a fine sieve to remove bubbles and pour into baking cups.

Sprinkle custard with ground nutmeg and put into oven. It is easy to overbake custard but important not to, for it will curdle. Custard is done when the center quivers and has not solidified, 45–60 minutes.

Remove custard from oven and cool. It will continue to bake a little more out of the oven.

# Vanilla Ice Cream

8 servings

This receipt calls for the use of a hand-crank ice cream maker.

The only way to know what ice cream tasted like prior to the invention of modern refrigeration is to churn it by hand. This is the kind of ice cream Tasha grew up with, and continued to make throughout her life. She often added fresh chopped peaches or strawberries to this receipt. A highlight of birthdays or a hot Sunday in July was the presentation of this simple ice cream. This receipt may explain how ice cream came by its name.

4 cups heavy cream

1½ cups sugar

¼ teaspoon salt

4 cups milk

1 tablespoon vanilla

In a saucepan, bring heavy cream nearly to a boil and then remove from heat. Mix in sugar and salt.

Chill overnight or for several hours, then add milk and vanilla. Pour custard into ice cream maker can. Pack freezer with ice and salt.

Crank slowly for the first 5 minutes. Ice cream is done when it becomes difficult to turn the crank.

# Oatmeal Cookies

## Makes 3 dozen 3–inch cookies

In New England a lot of snow typically falls in late February, through March, into April and occasionally even the beginning of May. By then there has been more than six months of winter, and Tasha would start quoting Mark Twain: "New England has nine months of winter and three months of bad sledding." And: "If you don't like the weather in New England, just wait a few minutes." Tasha worried about her garden during cold weather when there was not a lot of snow to insulate it. The dramatic rise and fall of temperatures as winter transitions to spring often thaws and refreezes the ground, which expands and rises, often destroying plants. An abrupt change in weather often precipitated a teatime treat. Early spring brought snow, rain, crocus, and oatmeal cookies.

| | |
|---|---|
| 1 cup soft butter | 2 cups all-purpose flour |
| 1 cup sugar | 1 teaspoon salt |
| 1 cup brown sugar, packed | 1 teaspoon baking soda |
| 2 eggs | 1 teaspoon cinnamon |
| 1 teaspoon vanilla | 3 cups quick rolled oats |

Preheat oven to 350°F.

In a large mixing bowl, combine butter, sugar, brown sugar, eggs, and vanilla.

Add flour, salt, baking soda, cinnamon, and oats. Mix until just combined.

Scoop the cookie dough out and onto baking sheet with a tablespoon. Use a fork to gently flatten the dough.

Bake 8 minutes or until cookies begin to brown on top.

Occasionally, Tasha added a cup of raisins to the dough, but that was rare.

# Pumpkin Pie

8 servings

Tasha did not often make pumpkin pies, but when she did they were particularly good. She made pies with small, smooth-skinned baking pumpkins, or butternut squash. Both grow well in her vegetable garden as long as a late spring frost doesn't visit in the night. Around dusk each day during the growing season she would walk through her gardens to give them a final check. She often went barefoot, and if the dew was especially cold on her feet she covered plants sensitive to frost with sheets, upside-down baskets, or her apron.

PIE SHELL:
1 cup sifted all-purpose flour
½ teaspoon salt

⅓ cup plus 1 tablespoon shortening
2 tablespoons ice water

FILLING:
1½ cups cooked pumpkin
1½ cups heavy cream
¾ cup sugar
½ teaspoon salt

1 teaspoon cinnamon
½ teaspoon ginger
¼ teaspoon ground cloves
2 eggs

To make the pie shell, mix flour and salt. Dump in shortening and cut into flour until size of peas. Sprinkle with water and gather together. Press into ball, roll out on a lightly floured surface, and transfer to pie plate.

Preheat oven to 425°F.

To make the pie filling, cut small baking pumpkin into 2-inch chunks and bake in ¼ inch water, skin side up, 30–45 minutes or until soft.

Cool slightly, scrape pumpkin from rind, and work through sieve by stirring with a wooden spoon. Combine remaining ingredients and mix well.

Pour into pie shell and bake at 425°F for 15 minutes, then 350°F for about 45 minutes or until fork inserted in center comes out clean. Cool for an hour or two and serve with whipped cream.

The Tasha Tudor Family Cookbook

# Rice Pudding

## 6 servings

The rice was stored in the blue cupboard on the second shelf from the top in the container it came in, next to boxes of tapioca, light brown sugar, confectioners' sugar, and raisins. Next to the box of regular raisins there was often a box of golden raisins, currants, and dried apricots. Rice pudding was a treat exclusive to winter. Occasionally Tasha put in raisins, but generally not too many. It seemed as though rice pudding cooked itself in her house, as it just appeared at the back of the stove around supper.

½ cup water

¾ cup white rice

⅓ teaspoon salt

4 cups milk

½ cup sugar

1 teaspoon vanilla

Bring water to boil and add rice and salt. Cook until water is absorbed, about 10 minutes.

Add milk and sugar. Stir frequently over medium heat for ½ hour or until ingredients begin to thicken. Stir in vanilla.

Overcooked rice pudding becomes solid when cool. It is just right when it remains creamy.

Serve with whipped cream and a dash of nutmeg or cinnamon.

# Snow Ice Cream

## 1 serving

Nowadays this is called ice cream on snow, or snow cone. Tasha called it snow ice cream. She also poured raspberry juice over a bowl of fresh snow in lieu of sugar, cream, and vanilla. This was strictly winter fare, and went hand in hand with snow lanterns, snow horses, snowshoeing, skiing, and snowstorms. A snow lantern is a small, hollow pyramidal cone constructed of snowballs with a lit candle in the interior. A snow horse is a horse or whole herd of horses constructed of snow the right size for children to ride.

Bowl of snow

½ cup heavy cream

3 tablespoons sugar

½ teaspoon vanilla

In a medium mixing bowl stir together cream, sugar, and vanilla. Locate a patch of fresh snow and scoop into a serving bowl. Pour contents of mixing bowl over snow and serve immediately.

# Speckled Cookies

### Makes 3–4 dozen cookies

Over the years, the most common cookie in the house was what Tasha called a speckled cookie. It is her version of spekulatius, a spiced cookie of Pennsylvanian origin. She kept a steady supply in the glass cookie jars that sit on the kitchen cupboard opposite the door that opens into the main house. Two jars held plain cookies, while the third contained sandwich cookies. To make a sandwich cookie, a layer of melted semisweet chocolate chips is applied between two speckled cookies. The assembly of sandwich cookies often fell to visitors. Tasha sat them at the end of the table with a pot of melted chocolate, stack of cookies, spoon, and sheet of wax paper while she prepared tea or supper, all the while carrying on memorable conversation.

1 pound butter

2 eggs

5 cups all-purpose flour

2 cups sugar

A little salt

1 teaspoon baking soda dissolved in 2–3 tablespoons milk

1–2 teaspoons cinnamon

¼ teaspoon cloves

Dump all ingredients in bowl and mix by hand until smooth dough is formed. Chill in refrigerator 2 hours.

Preheat oven to 350°F.

Roll dough to ⅛-inch thickness. A 2-inch fluted cookie cutter makes about 3–4 dozen.

Bake for 8–10 minutes.

# Quick Yellow Cake

## 12 servings

This is a cross between a yellow cake and a white cake and was often made when there was a lot to do and not enough time to do it. Tasha baked with cake pans with removable bottoms. She left the removable cake pan bottom on in this receipt, which seemed to facilitate the frosting and transportation of a freshly baked cake. Often she frosted it before it cooled completely. Slightly melted chocolate frosting, combined with warm vanilla pudding in between a warm layer cake, was the hallmark of this confection. If in a real hurry, she only frosted the top, with extra-thick chocolate frosting.

CAKE:
3½ cups all-purpose flour
1 tablespoon baking powder
½ teaspoon salt
1 cup milk

1 teaspoon vanilla
2 sticks butter
2 cups sugar
4 eggs

CHOCOLATE FROSTING:
6 tablespoons butter, melted
2⅔ cups confectioners' sugar
½ cup baking cocoa

1 teaspoon vanilla
⅓ cup milk

Preheat oven to 350°F.

In a large bowl, mix flour, baking powder, and salt. Add milk, vanilla, butter, sugar, and eggs. Stir until smooth, then pour into two round greased 9-inch cake pans.

Bake 25–30 minutes or until toothpick inserted in middle comes out clean.

To make the frosting, combine all ingredients in bowl and mix thoroughly.

# Beverages

# Tea

## 4–6 servings

Every afternoon Tasha set out a teapot, creamer, sugar bowl, cups, and saucers, and put the teakettle on to heat. If she expected more than three or four visitors, she used two teapots and put out an extra plate of crackers or cookies. Once everyone was settled, she lit the beeswax candles, poured the tea, inquired if milk or sugar was desired, and if so how much, then settled in her usual spot. She sat in a rocking chair with a black woolen blanket over the back and a blue-check pillow cushion on the seat. She used a cup without a handle and warmed both hands with it. The coziest teatimes occurred in winter by the woodstove, and in familiar company Tasha propped her feet on the fender. There was always a background of corgi dogs pattering about, canaries singing, the grandfather clock chiming every half hour, the cat purring or a teakettle coming to boil, the soft gleam of candlelight on copper, and the scent of herbs drying and fresh-baked bread or cookies. Tasha did much of her correspondence from this spot, and kept a few art pencils and erasers on the little table beside her chair. The corgis loved to chew those erasers if they fell to the floor.

Prepare the teapot by filling with hot tap water. Bring fresh, cold water to a rolling boil.

Empty the teapot and add 1 teaspoonful of tea for each cup and an additional one for the pot. Fill the teapot with boiling water and allow to steep 3–5 minutes. Stir once, then let the tea settle.

If you wish for weaker or stronger tea, adjust the amount of tea, not the brewing time.

# Hot Cider

## 8 servings

All year, except late summer, the cider press sits in the woodshed adjacent to the passageway leading into the house. The door beside it is apt to flap around in the wind that comes in from the south. Tasha tied a length of string through the door handle and looped the other end over the cider press, and as a consequence the press is still useful in the off-season. Setting up the cider press is a yearly ritual. Children, especially, enjoy collecting apples and watching them turn into cider. The most exciting moment occurs when ground-up apples are pressed and cider pours into a waiting cup. A bushel of apples yields about three gallons of cider. Occasionally Tasha made cider from apples peeled and cored, which made a delicate and delicious beverage. During years when the apple trees around the house did not produce much fruit, Tasha drove to nearby orchards to obtain apples. She filled bushel baskets and set them in the trunk and backseat. She did not own many cars during her life. From the 1960s onwards she drove an old Land Rover that required frequent repair, then a small green Toyota pickup, onward a green Volvo sedan. That's not to say she didn't do much driving. She did, and with those cars.

Tasha stored apples in the dairy. She served hot cider mostly on Thanksgiving and Christmas.

2 quarts apple cider

2 cinnamon sticks

2 whole allspice

1 teaspoon whole cloves

¼ teaspoon ground nutmeg

Combine all ingredients in large pot, heat to just below boiling, and simmer for 10 minutes. Pour through strainer to remove spices.

# Hot Lemon Tea

1 serving

This is a drink Tasha made to soothe sore throats. In addition to keeping a large supply of grapefruits and oranges, she kept on hand a half dozen each of lemons and limes for flavoring fish, adding to desserts, or using in tea. She stored them sealed in a plastic bag in the refrigerator, which kept them fresh for several weeks. Occasionally a lemon would be lost in the back of the refrigerator for a while and dry out. Tasha cut it into quarters and froze it for later use in drinks.

1 cup water

1–2 teaspoons honey

1 tablespoon fresh lemon juice

Heat water to near boiling and stir in honey and lemon juice.

# Orange Juice

## 1 serving

Each morning Tasha cut an orange in half and squeezed out the juice with an old glass juicer. It took not more than a minute to do, and she maintained there was no comparison between freshly squeezed and the alternative. Sometimes she didn't finish the orange juice right away, but kept it beside her paintbrushes while she worked. Every year Tasha signed up for a seasonal delivery of oranges and grapefruits. On the first of each month the mailman left a large white box containing oranges and grapefruits in the outbuilding at the end of Tasha's driveway. Back then, the half-mile driveway was not plowed. She stored them on the back stair landing adjacent to the kitchen. By the time four weeks had passed the box was about empty.

1 orange

Take 1 uncut orange and press briefly but firmly against counter with palm of hand. Cut orange in half along equator. Squeeze the juice from each half with a hand juicer. Pour through a strainer into a cup, or omit strainer if pulp is desired.

# Root Beer

## 16 servings

Once a year on a warm, sunny summer day, Tasha assembled a box of bottle caps and a few dozen brown glass bottles and made root beer on the front porch. It was seldom a solitary endeavor, and quite a lot of planning went into it. The root beer does not taste like the commercial product, and each batch is apt to taste a bit different because of variations in the fermentation process. This is a receipt that requires familiarity.

| | |
|---|---|
| 4 quarts water | ½ teaspoon ground nutmeg |
| ¼ teaspoon brewer's yeast | 10 whole allspice, crushed |
| 2 tablespoons licorice root | 1 tablespoon lemon juice |
| 6 whole cloves, crushed | 1 tablespoon wintergreen leaves |
| 2 cinnamon sticks | ¼ cup molasses |
| 2 vanilla beans | 1 cup packed brown sugar |

Boil ¼ cup water, let cool to 90°F, and stir in yeast. Let stand 10–15 minutes.

In a large pot add water, licorice, cloves, cinnamon, vanilla, nutmeg, allspice, lemon juice, and wintergreen leaves. Bring to a boil, then simmer for 20 minutes. Stir in molasses and sugar and simmer for 10 minutes. Remove from heat and cool to 75°F.

Strain through cheesecloth to remove spices. Stir in yeast and fill bottles immediately, leaving a 2-inch space at the top of each bottle. Cap the bottles and store horizontally in a warm location (around 70°F) between 2–4 days to allow carbonation. Remove to refrigerator to slow carbonation. Keep refrigerated and use up after a week or two. As it ferments, a bottle of root beer builds pressure and may explode.

# Rose Hip Tea

## 4–6 servings

Rose hip tea was a seasonal treat for Tasha. There are many dozens of roses growing in her garden, all of which form rose hips ranging from yellow and orange to bright red as summer tips toward autumn. She selected rosehips that were firm, bright, large, and otherwise appealing to the eye. Rose hips from *Rosa rugosa* fit that bill and were the primary candidates. Tasha typically cut the rose hips in half lengthwise, scraped out the seeds, and discarded them in the compost. She first poured hot water into a large teapot to let it warm, dumped out the water, added the rose hips to the empty pot, and finally poured in boiling water. This tea is mild, fruity, rich in vitamin C, and best made from fresh rose hips.

¼ cup rose hips

1 quart water

Bring water to a boil, add rose hips, and steep 10–20 minutes. Leave rose hips in pot. If desired, use a small strainer when pouring tea.

# Stillwater Tea

## 14–20 servings

This beverage is one of Tasha's specialties. She made it from late spring through late summer, most frequently on the hottest days of the year, usually from July into August. She set the front porch table with a turkey-red tablecloth, straw spoons, cups, sugar water, a plate of cookies, and a vase of flowers.

| | |
|---|---|
| 1 cup sugar | 6 oranges |
| ¼ cup water | 6 lemons |
| 5 tablespoons black loose-leaf tea | 6 limes |
| 1 quart fresh cold water | 1 quart ginger ale |

Make a simple syrup by bringing sugar and ¼ cup water to a boil, then reducing heat and simmering until sugar dissolves. Cool, then place in a canning jar with a lid, but don't refrigerate or it will crystallize.

Pour 1 quart boiling water into a pitcher with 5 tablespoons tea leaves and steep 5 minutes, stirring once. Pour tea through strainer into second pitcher. Cool but don't refrigerate, as doing so will cloud tea.

Juice the oranges, lemons, and limes. For each serving, put fruit juice in a large glass, pour tea to halfway mark, then fill remainder with ginger ale and 2 ice cubes. Add syrup to taste. Garnish with mint.

# Conversion Charts

## METRIC AND IMPERIAL CONVERSIONS

(These conversions are rounded for convenience)

| Ingredient | Cups/Tablespoons/ Teaspoons | Ounces | Grams/Milliliters |
|---|---|---|---|
| Butter | 1 cup=16 tablespoons= 2 sticks | 8 ounces | 230 grams |
| Cream cheese | 1 tablespoon | 0.5 ounce | 14.5 grams |
| Cheese, shredded | 1 cup | 4 ounces | 110 grams |
| Cornstarch | 1 tablespoon | 0.3 ounce | 8 grams |
| Flour, all-purpose | 1 cup/1 tablespoon | 4.5 ounces/0.3 ounce | 125 grams/8 grams |
| Flour, whole wheat | 1 cup | 4 ounces | 120 grams |
| Fruit, dried | 1 cup | 4 ounces | 120 grams |
| Fruits or veggies, chopped | 1 cup | 5 to 7 ounces | 145 to 200 grams |
| Fruits or veggies, puréed | 1 cup | 8.5 ounces | 245 grams |
| Honey, maple syrup, or corn syrup | 1 tablespoon | .75 ounce | 20 grams |
| Liquids: cream, milk, water, or juice | 1 cup | 8 fluid ounces | 240 milliliters |
| Oats | 1 cup | 5.5 ounces | 150 grams |
| Salt | 1 teaspoon | 0.2 ounce | 6 grams |
| Spices: cinnamon, cloves, ginger, or nutmeg (ground) | 1 teaspoon | 0.2 ounce | 5 milliliters |
| Sugar, brown, firmly packed | 1 cup | 7 ounces | 200 grams |
| Sugar, white | 1 cup/1 tablespoon | 7 ounces/0.5 ounce | 200 grams/12.5 grams |
| Vanilla extract | 1 teaspoon | 0.2 ounce | 4 grams |

## OVEN TEMPERATURES

| Fahrenheit | Celsius | Gas Mark |
|---|---|---|
| 225° | 110° | ¼ |
| 250° | 120° | ½ |
| 275° | 140° | 1 |
| 300° | 150° | 2 |
| 325° | 160° | 3 |
| 350° | 180° | 4 |
| 375° | 190° | 5 |
| 400° | 200° | 6 |
| 425° | 220° | 7 |
| 450° | 230° | 8 |

# Index

Winslow Tudor

The Tasha Tudor Family Cookbook